AN EYEBALL, BIG, YELLOWISH, DISTINCTLY INHUMAN, STARES RAPTLY

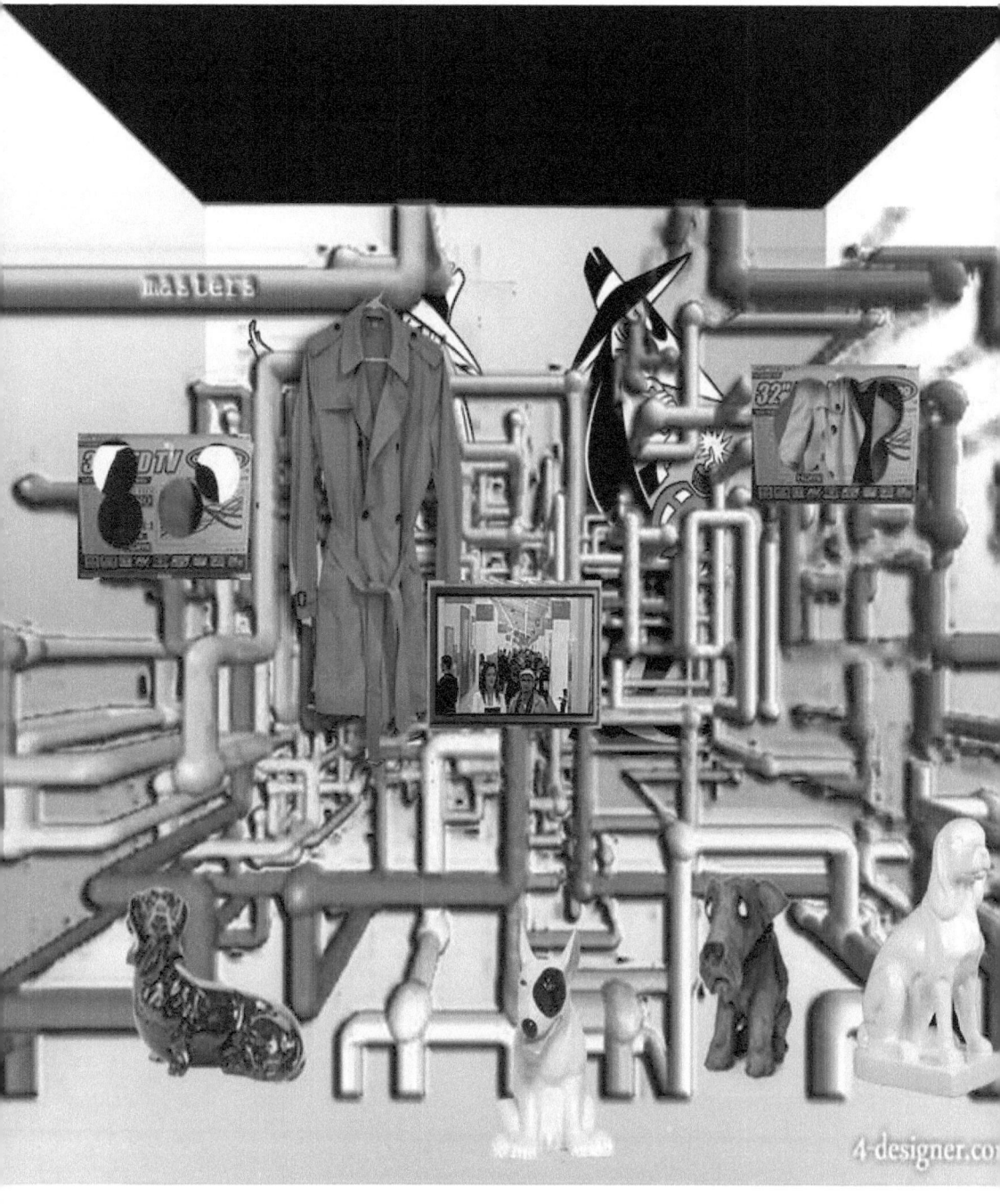

I changed some things up with the booth but basically coat hangers based off that old pc screensaver that the screens were also mounted to. any thoughts?

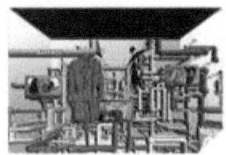

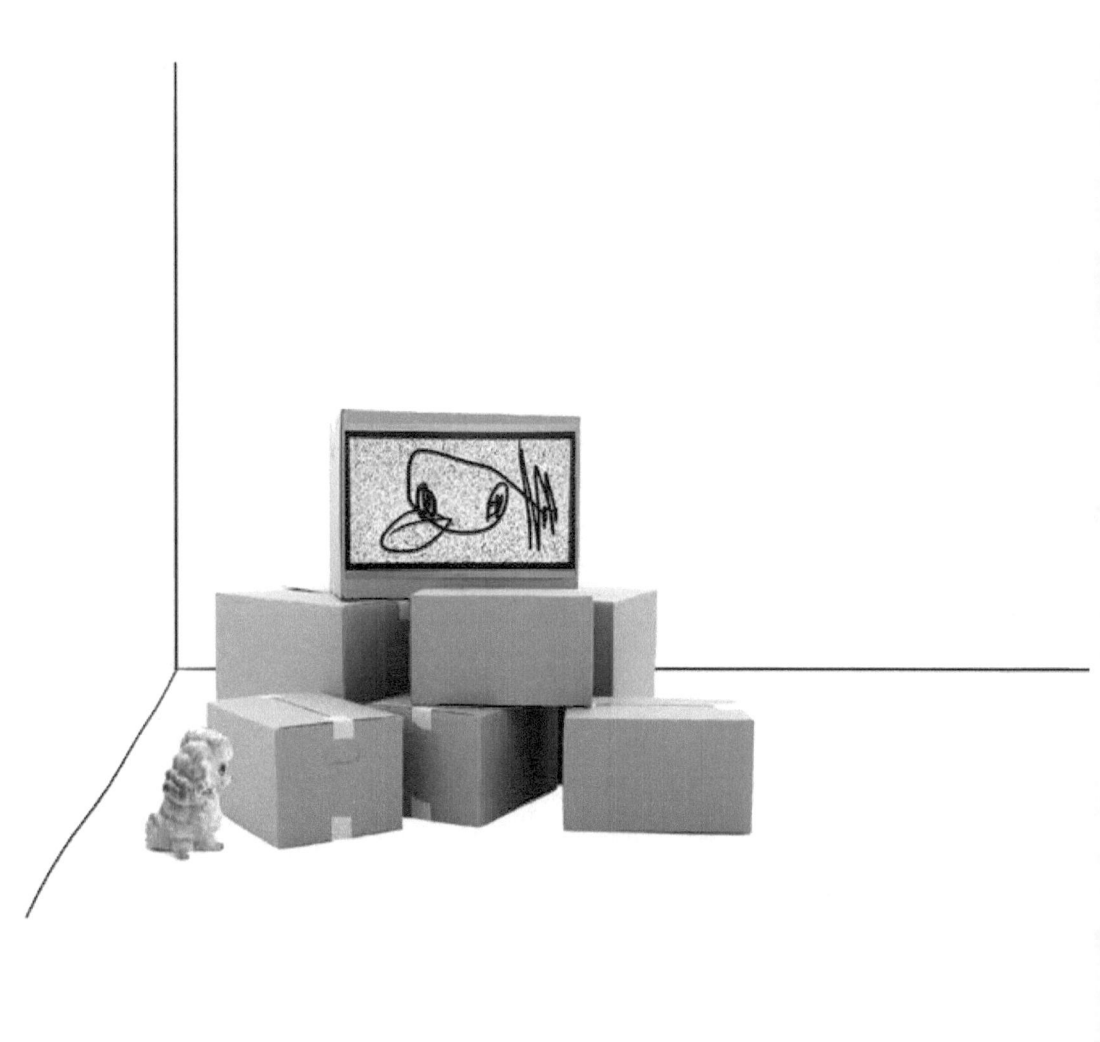

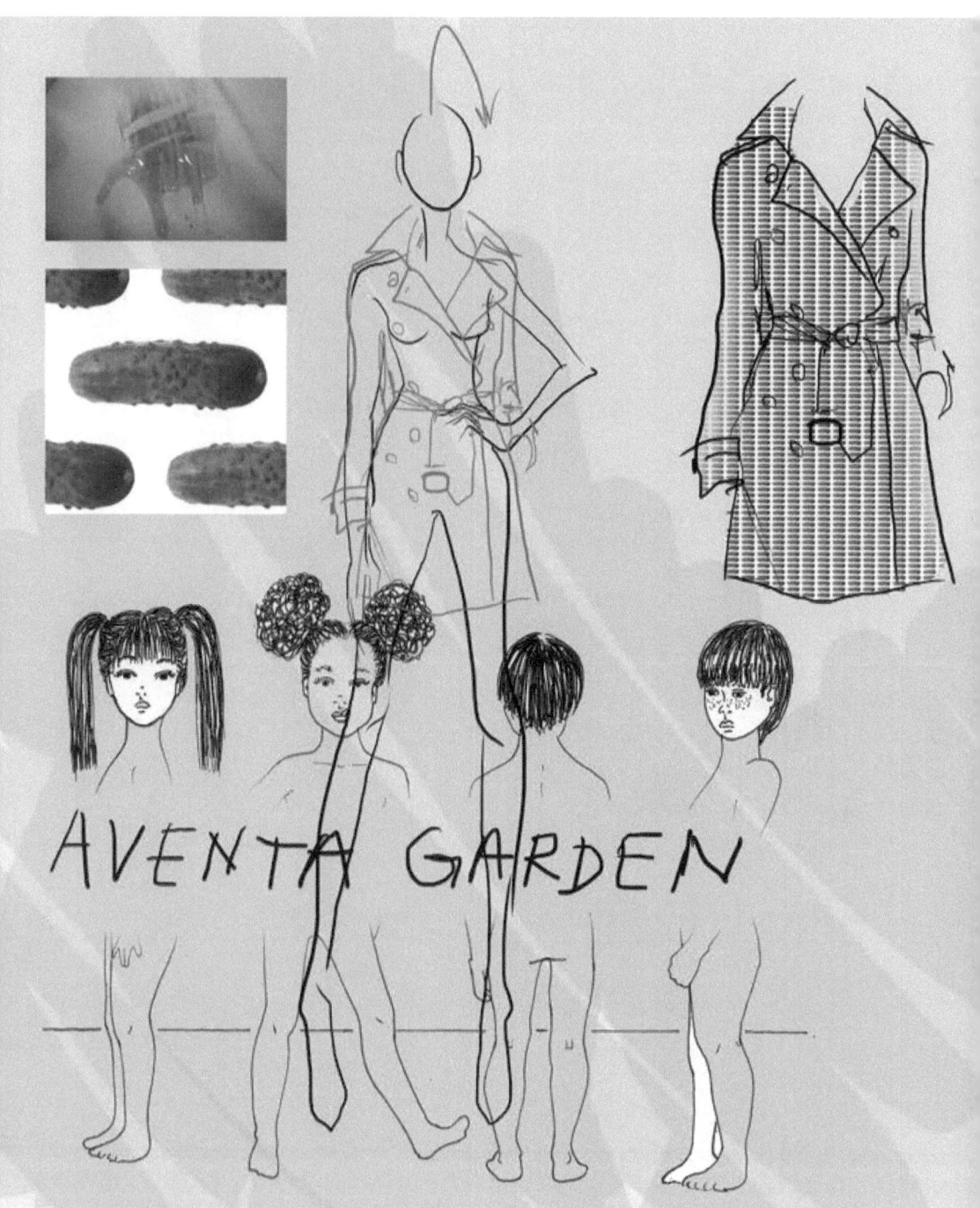

AVENTA GARDEN

Champagne Poppin <bodybybody@gmail.com> Sep 4 (4 days ago)

to Liv, Parker, Nelson

Hey guys,

These are pretty crappy... maybe parker can scribble on them? :-/

<3

C+M

2 Attachments

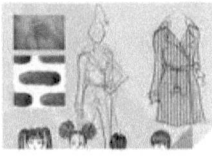 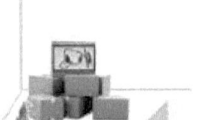

Liv Barrett Sep 3 (6 days ago) ☆
to me, Parker, Nelson ▾

BxB,

do you think you'd be able to work on a sketch for the fair booth? as best that you can visually project.
judging by the advice I've just received (11th hour, albeit), any visual suggestions of the work being proposed are only helpful. I also somehow imagine that illustrations of the trench coats produced by you would be brilliant.

maybe one sketch of the booth and one of the possible trench coats?

your superb and convincing illustrations skills would be magnificent. the footprint of the stand is 5x5 metres, so 15x15 feet.

call if u want to chat or have questions

xxx

millions of kisses
_____

Champagne Poppin <bodybybody@gmail.com>   Sep 6 (3 days ago)

to Bea

That sounds great! We definitely want to use the prosthetics. I'm curious about the disease look, can you elaborate on that or do you have some examples?

 We'll get you some more images/drawings of what we are looking for specifically. We'll also check with the photographer what day works best for them and get back to you asap.

Thanks again,
Cameron and Melissa

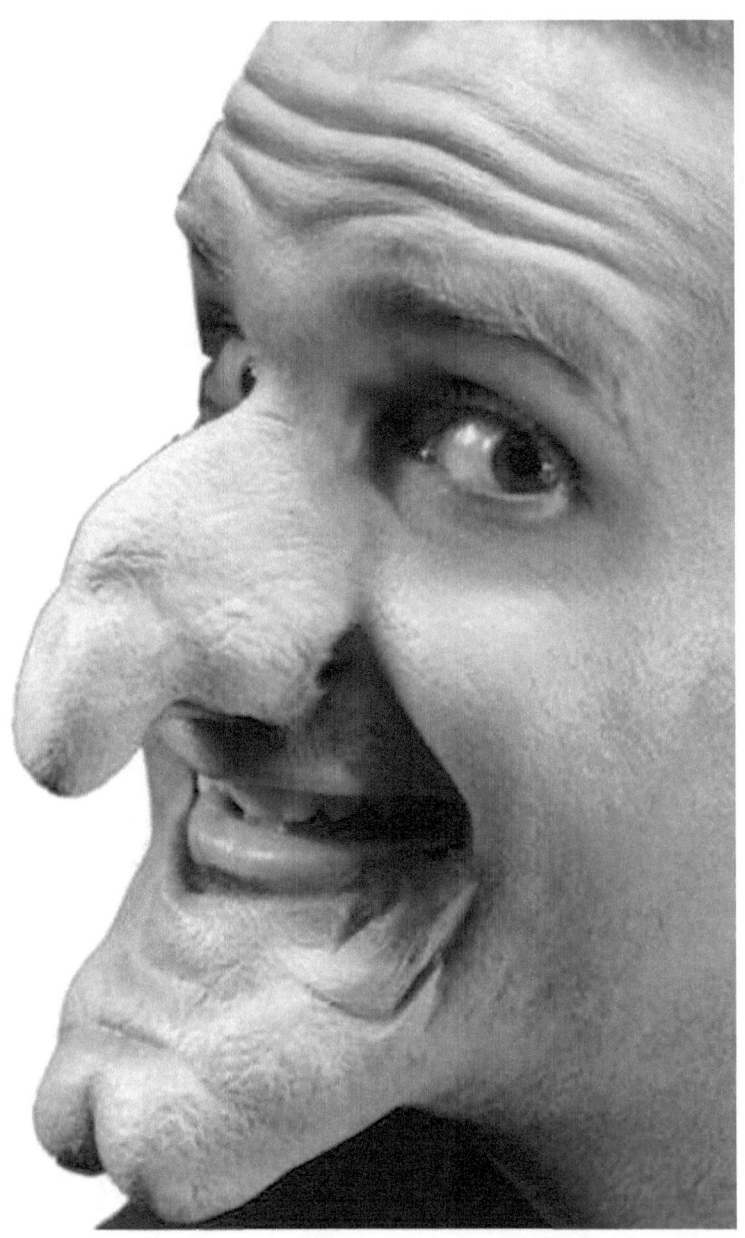

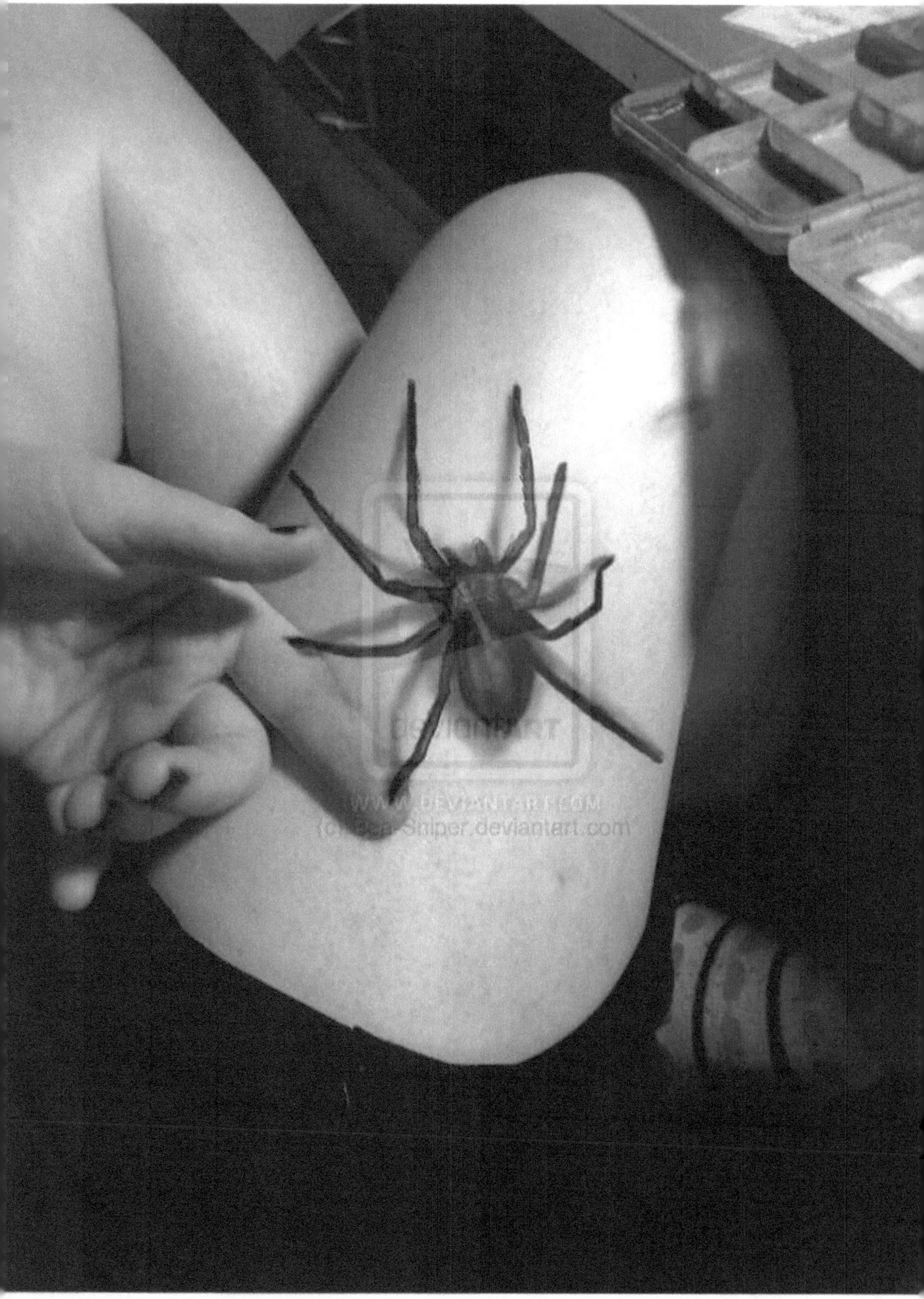
WWW.DEVIANTART.COM

Hi,

We came across your contact information hrough a link on your production hub profile and were interested in getting a quote from you to do special fx makeup on two individuals (just faces). We would need these done relatively soon, in the next two weeks. How does pricing normally work? Is it hourly or determined by the amount of detail?

Let us know if this is something you would be available to do, what you need from us for a rough estimate and we can send you more details.

Thanks!
Cameron and Melissa

I would definitely be able to do this.
Pricing depends on what you want done. If it involved prosthetics, the material has different pricing too.
You have to tell me a bit more about what youd like done. I'd be more than happy to help! :)

Respectfully,

Champagne Poppin <bodybybody@gmail.com>   Sep 6 (3 days ago)

to beatricesniper

Hi,

We came across your contact information hrough a link on your production hub profile and were interested in getting a quote from you to do special fx makeup on two individuals (just faces). We would need these done relatively soon, in the next two weeks. How does pricing normally work? Is it hourly or determined by the amount of detail?

Let us know if this is something you would be available to do, what you need from us for a rough estimate and we can send you more details.

Thanks!
Cameron and Melissa

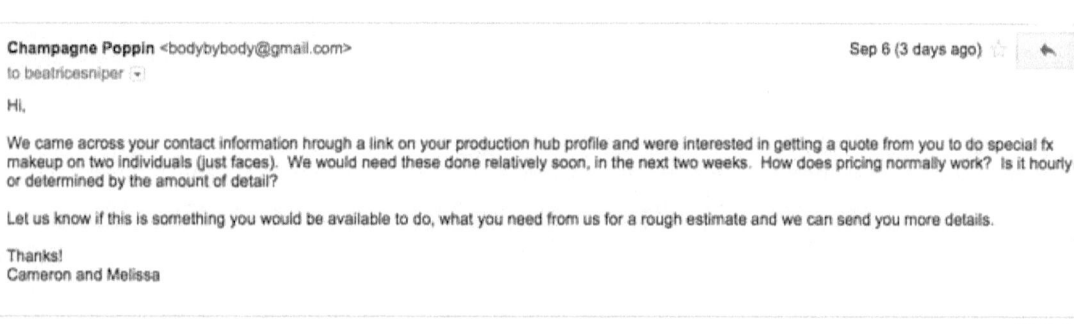

Bea   Sep 6 (3 days ago)

to me

I would definitely be able to do this.
Pricing depends on what you want done. If it involved prosthetics, the material has different pricing too.
You have to tell me a bit more about what youd like done. I'd be more than happy to help! :)

Respectfully,

noreply@lulu.com   7:14 PM (20 minute

to me

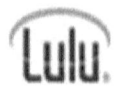

Dear Cameron Soren,

This automated email was sent because you requested a password reset for your Lulu account.

To reset your password, please click the link below:

https://lulu.com/account/password-reset/66102726/hCRZZSHLWljLa78FQoUVlg

If clicking the link does not work, please copy and paste the URL in a new browser window. If you did not initiate this request, you ca
message.

Thanks for your support,

Your friends at Lulu Press, Inc.

ISBN assigned to book, "TRYING TO MAKE A SPREAD FOR ART PAPERS"

Lulu <isbn@lulu.com>
to me

7:19 PM (13 minutes ago)

An ISBN has been assigned to your book

ISBN #: 978-1-312-50366-3

Content ID: 15223585

Book Title: TRYING TO MAKE A SPREAD FOR ART PAPERS

===
Next Steps:
===

- Add your ISBN to the copyright page of your book.

- If you design and upload your own book cover, add your ISBN to the
back cover of your design. If you use Lulu's cover design tool, we
will add your ISBN to the back cover automatically.

- Check out our distribution requirements and format your book accordingly:
http://www.lulu.com/services/distribution/globalreach

- Once you've published your book, get globalREACH distribution for free.
This is the distribution service for your book to be listed on retail channels,
such as Amazon.com, BN.com and in major bibliographic databases. You can view
the eligible size, binding, ink and page count options for globalREACH here:
http://www.lulu.com/services/distribution/globalreach

Upon adding a distribution service to your book, you will receive instructions on
completing your book's submission to our distribution partners.

===

Lulu Press, Inc.

3101 Hillsborough St, Raleigh, NC 27607

www.lulu.com

I think that's totally doable. Only thing is the draft will mainly be a storyboard, or all of the non-photo elements since next week we'll still be sorting and photoshopping the photos...

and yeah, hit us up when you're in town and we can meet up!

Cam

Hey,

Sorry for silence this weekend - we had an opening in ATL and I was installing and then in a coma.

Need draft in a week and final on the 26th. Doable?

Let me know if you want to chat anything out this week.

Also I am in NY Sept 16-18 and again Sept 24-29 for the book fair.

If you guys want to meet mid-month we can pow wow in my mother's weird union square bachelor pad.

V

Sent from my iPhone

Cameron Soren <cameronsoren@gmail.com>

to Victoria

An update

We're still sticking with the comic book idea but instead of being entirely drawings we're hiring a special fx makeup artist to add prosthetics to our faces. She seems really good from what we've seen of her portfolio. I might have some sort of butt-hole for a mouth and a really exaggerated chin.   We're going to use these photos of us with prosthetics as the characters in the comic...trying to shoot it next week.

will get you a basic storyboard asap

seamless

Arepera Guacuco Restaurant

Phone: (347) 305-3300

Order #: 647237622   C

Ordered: Tuesday, September 09, 2014 5:47 PM

Estimated Delivery Time: 40 - 55 minutes

Deliver to:
Cameron Soren
18 Menahan St
Cross Streets: Bushwick Ave. and Evergreen Ave.
City: Brooklyn
Apt/Flat/Suite/Floor #: # 3L
(415) 568-1483

Delivery Instructions:
Do not include plastic utensils, napkins, etc.

1	**Pabellón Criollo**	$12.50	x 1 =	$12.90
	• Spicy Sauce	$0.40		

Product Total:	=	$12.90
Sales Tax:	=	$1.14
Tip Amount:	=	$2.00
Grand Total:	=	$16.04

Hi!
Quick question for you, we're trying to schedule someone to help us out with one particular aspect of our spread and wanted to also get the date of when the final draft is due. I know draft is mid this month.

Hope all is well with you,
Thanks!

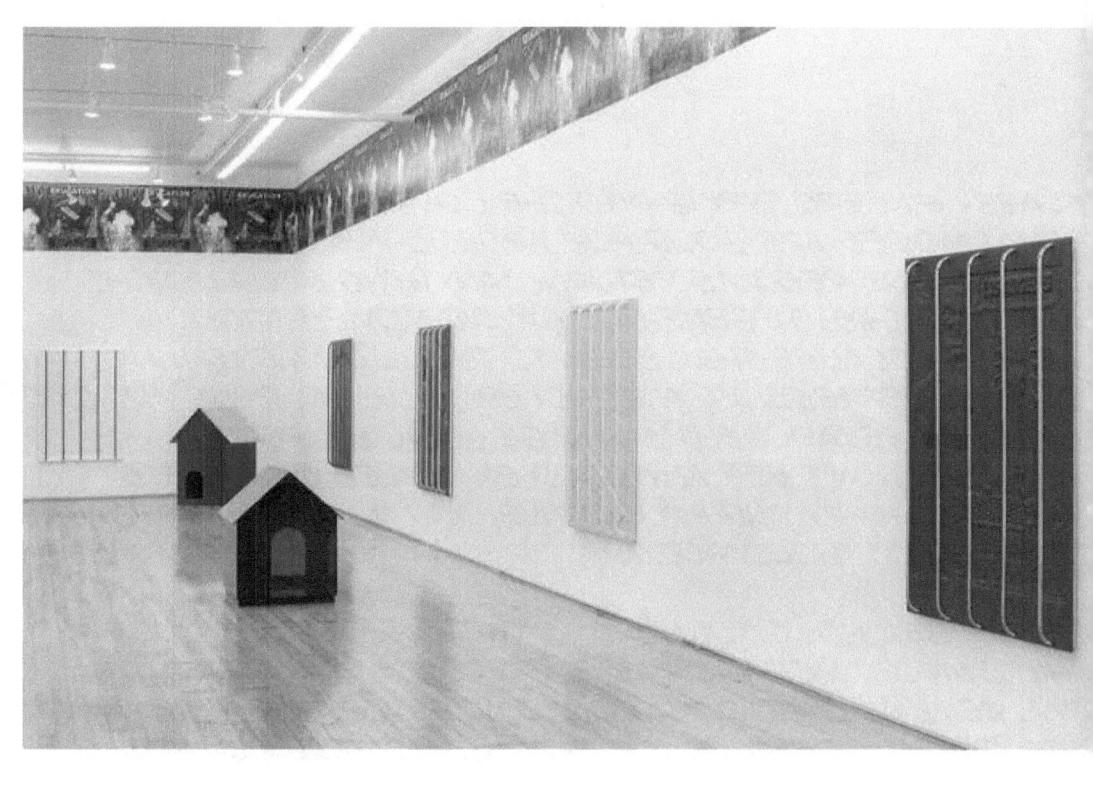

MELISSA STORMS INTO THE ROOM WEARING _____
"HEY, WE WERE SAVING THAT!"

CAMERON DOESN'T STIR. TWO OVERSIZED DRAWINGS ARE
STUFFED INSIDE HIS EARS. MELISSA IS SENSITIVE AT THE
MOMENT - THERE'S A DEADLINE FAST APPROACHING AND
NEITHER ONE OF THEM HAVE BEEN INSPIRED. THEY ARE A
FRAID TO LEAVE THEIR APARTMENT, FOR THE OUTSIDE WORLD

FLABBY FINGERS TYPING INTO THE COMPUTER SEARCH
"WHAT MOVIES ARE GOOD FOR ARTISTIC INSPIRATION".
THE OBVIOUS RESULTS RETURN: "ANYTHING DAVID LYNCH"
AND THEN THIS: "I GENERALLY AVOID MOVIES ABOUT
ARTISTS BECAUSE THEY SEEM TO DWELL ON MENTAL I
LLNESS, DEPRESSION, ALCOHOLISM, SUICIDE, DRUG ADDICTION
, ABUSIVE RELATIONSHIPS AND GENERAL STUPIDITY.
YOU JUST DON'T SEE ANY GOOD EXAMPLES OF ARTISTS
WHO ARE HAPPY AND PRODUCTIVE, AND NOT INSANE BECAUSE
 THAT IS NOT "HOLLYWOOD.""

"REMEMBER HOLY MOUNTAIN" CAMERON SQUEALS OUT OF
 HIS SWIRLED MOUTH ORIFICE.
"YA, REMEMBER HOW THAT ONCE WAS INSPIRING BUT NOW
 ITS JUST A CESSPOOL OF OBVIOUS SURREAL CLICHéS?
LE SIGH" "HAHAHA"

MELISSA CONTINUES TO SCROLL FURTHER DOWN UNTIL
SHE REACHES THIS COMMENT: RE: WHAT MOVIES ARE
GREAT FOR ARTISTIC INSPIRATION? SCHINDLERS LIST

"UGH WHAT IS WRONG WITH PEOPLE

AN EYEBALL, BIG, YELLOWISH, DISTINCTLY INHUMAN, STARES RAPTLY
BETWEEN WOODEN SLATS, PART OF A LARGE CRATE. THE EYE DARTS FROM SIDE
TO SIDE, ALERT AS HELL. (CLOSE UP OF THIS IMAGE IN CORNER OF PAGE - MAYBE TAKES PLACE IN WINDOW ACROSS FROM OUR APARTMENT IN ANOTHER BUILDING)

A LEGEND TRIES TO PLACE US -

-- BUT TO US IT'S STILL THE MIDDLE OF NOWHERE. COULD BE BOGOTA, COULD BE PILSEN, COULD BE HIGHLAND PARK.

IT'S QUIET FOR A SECOND. A ROAR RISES UP FROM THE STREET, DEAFENING. THE PIGEONS SCATTER AS SOMETHING VERY, VERY LARGE PLOWS AHEAD
THROUGH THEM, RIGHT AT US. ALAS, IT IS THE HORRIBLE SOUND OF THAT SONG, YOU KNOW THE APOCALYPTIC SLEEPER HIT NOW A CENTURY OLD ANTHEM FOR IMMORTAL YOUTH:

"I'M WAKING UP TO ASH AND DUST
I WIPE MY BROW AND I SWEAT MY RUST
I'M BREATHING IN THE CHEMICALS"

AS HE NORMALLY DOES, CAMERON PEERS OUT THE WINDOW IN THE FRONT OF THE APARTMENT OVERLOOKING THE CROWDE STREET (ONE ALLERGY-INFESTED WATERY EYEBALL PRESSED
IN BETWEEN TWO DUSTY WINDOW SLATS). THIS TIME HE FINDS A CHROME-DIPPED RAT DRAWN WAGON PLOWING DOWN MENAHAN WITH 2-STORY HIGH SPEAKERS ENCASED IN NEWLY DISTRESSED LEATHER. HE QUICKLY TURNS OUT THE LIGHTS, PLUGS HIS EARS WITH WHATEVER RANDOM EAR-SIZED OBJECT IS LYING ON THE FLOOR NEXT TO HIS SWOLLEN NIKE EMBLAZONED FEET, AND CLOSES HIS EYES ... WAITING FOR IT TO END.

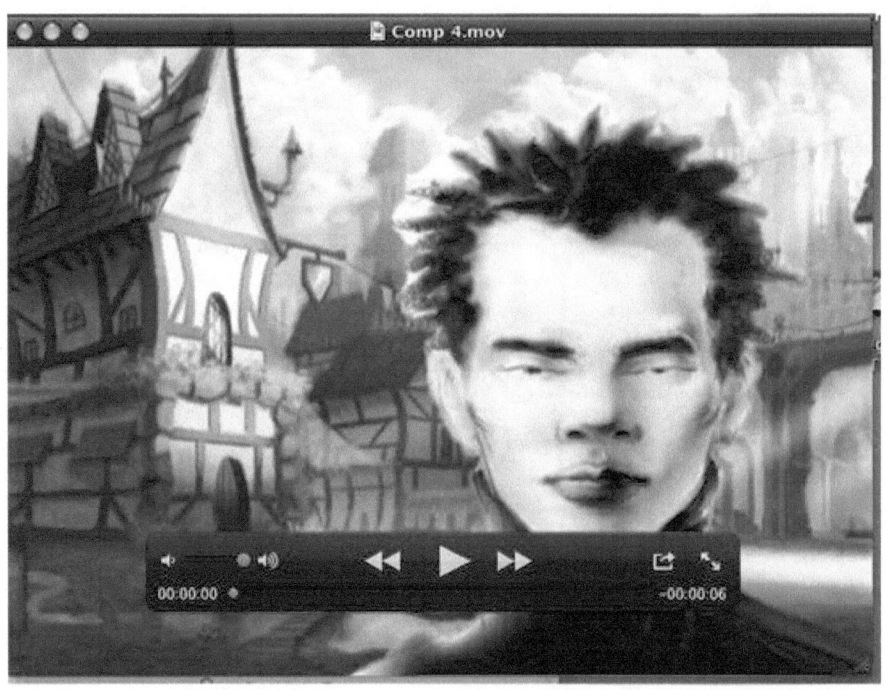

CAMERON SOREN 2014

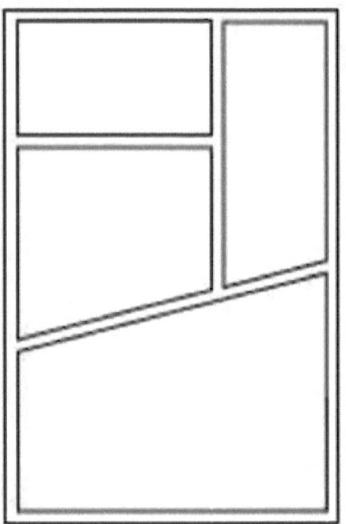

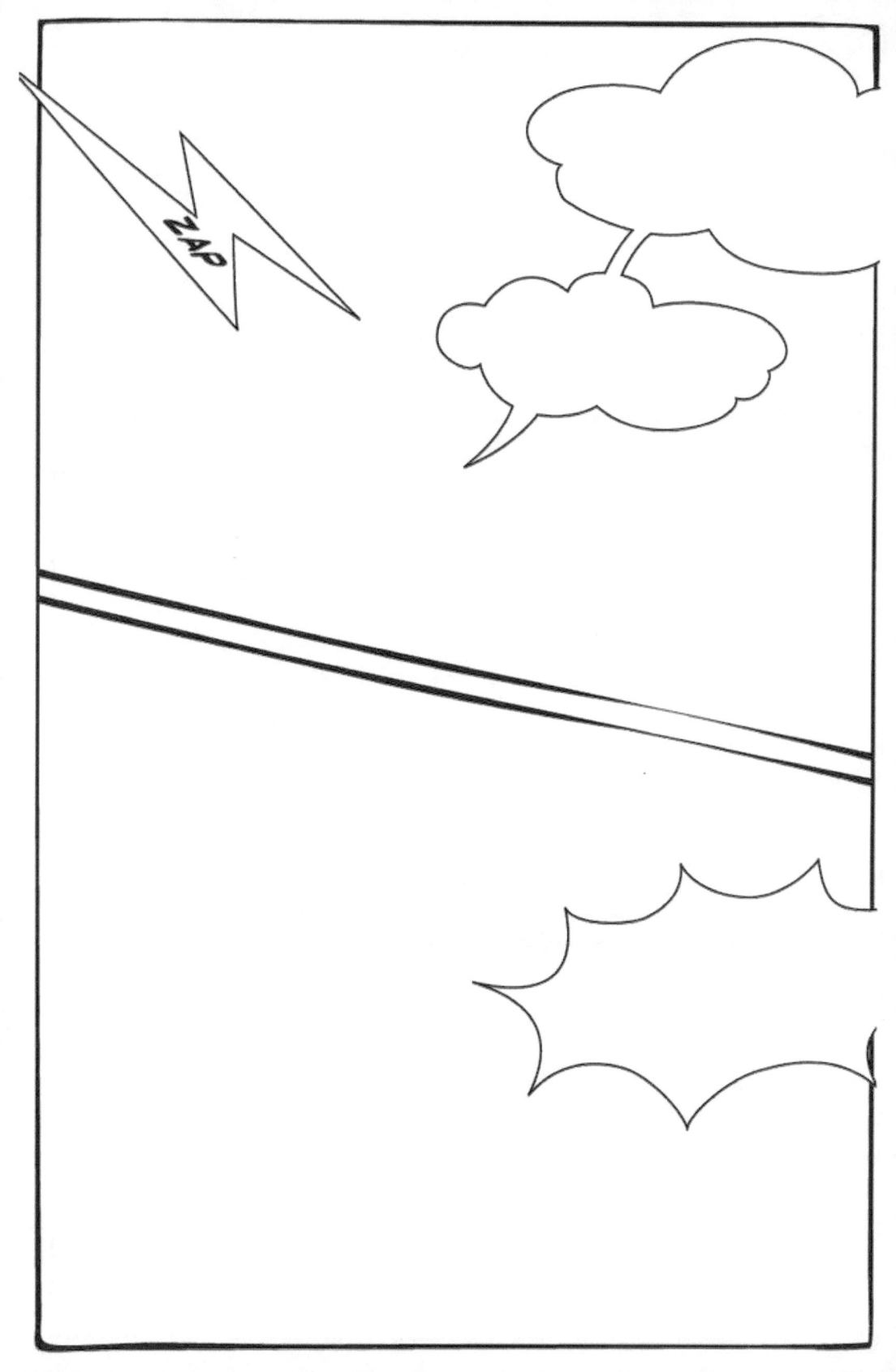

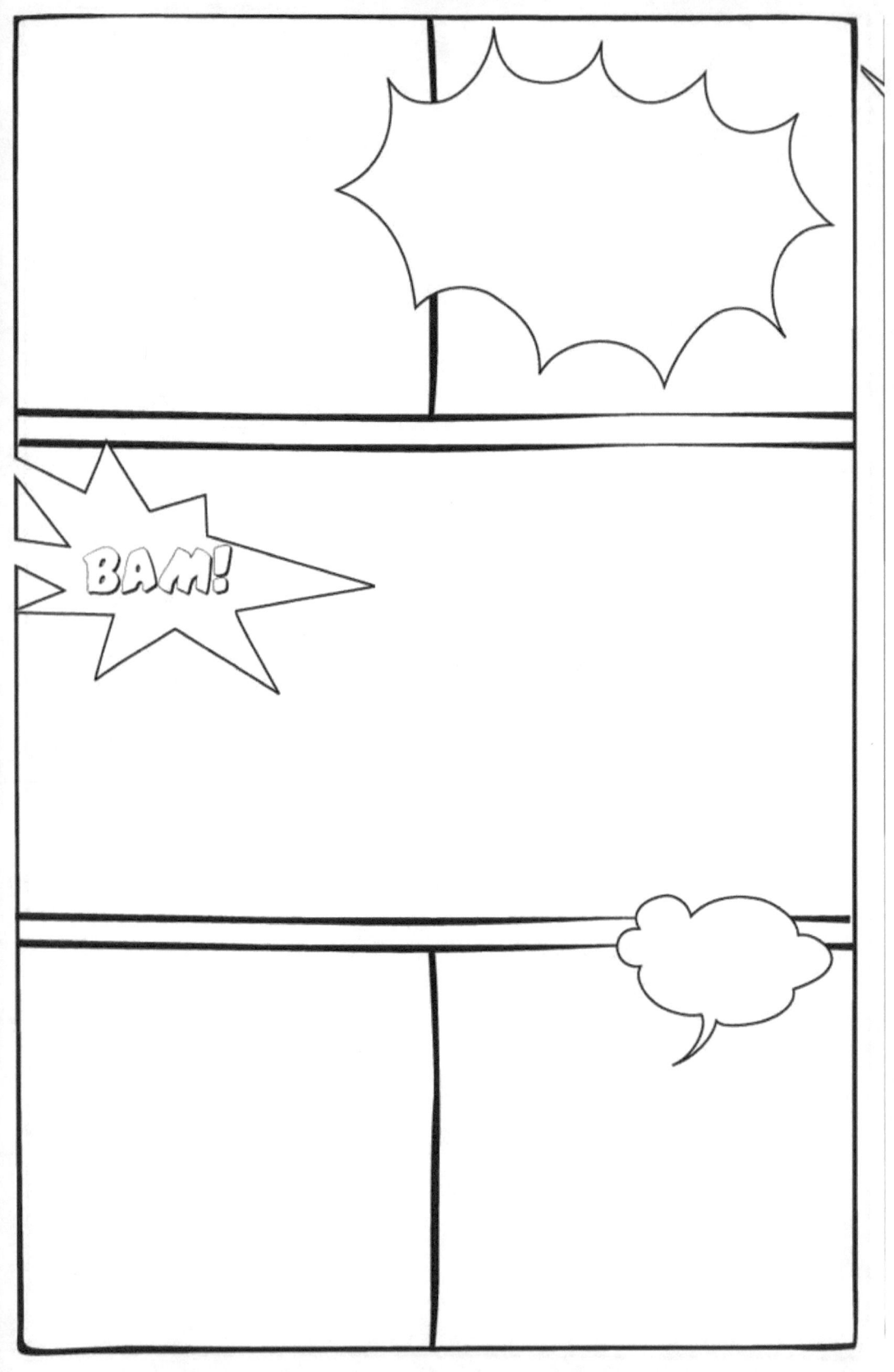

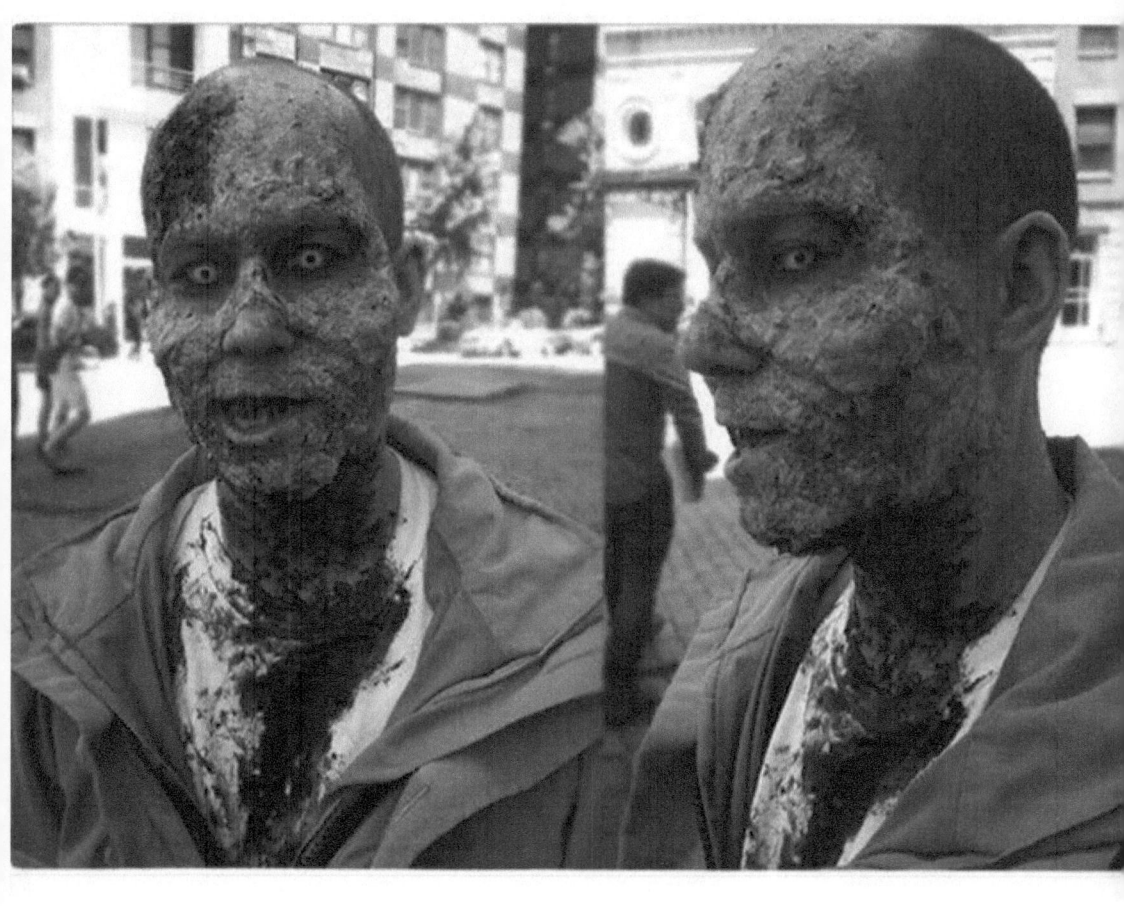

$15.56

Thanks for choosing Uber, Cameron

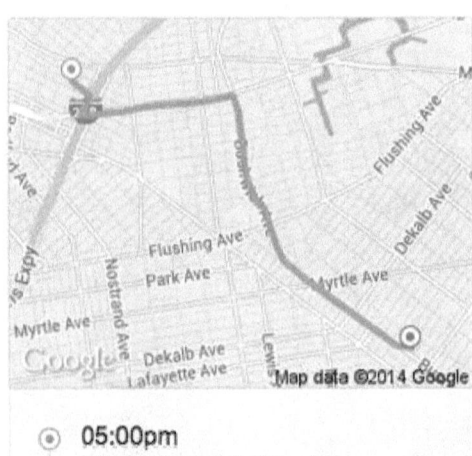

FARE BREAKDOWN

Base Fare	3.00
Distance	6.21
Time	6.35
Subtotal	**$15.56**

CHARGED
VISA Personal •••• 4402   **$15.56**

◉ **05:00pm**
289 Grand Street, Brooklyn, NY

◉ **05:15pm**
18 Menahan Street, Brooklyn, NY

hey bitch 　　 📭 　 Inbox x 　　　　　　　　　　　　　　　　　　　　　　　　🖨

Nate Miller　　　　　　　　　　　　　　　　　　　　　　　12:00 am (1 day ago) ☆　↩
to me ▾

need more tv to watch

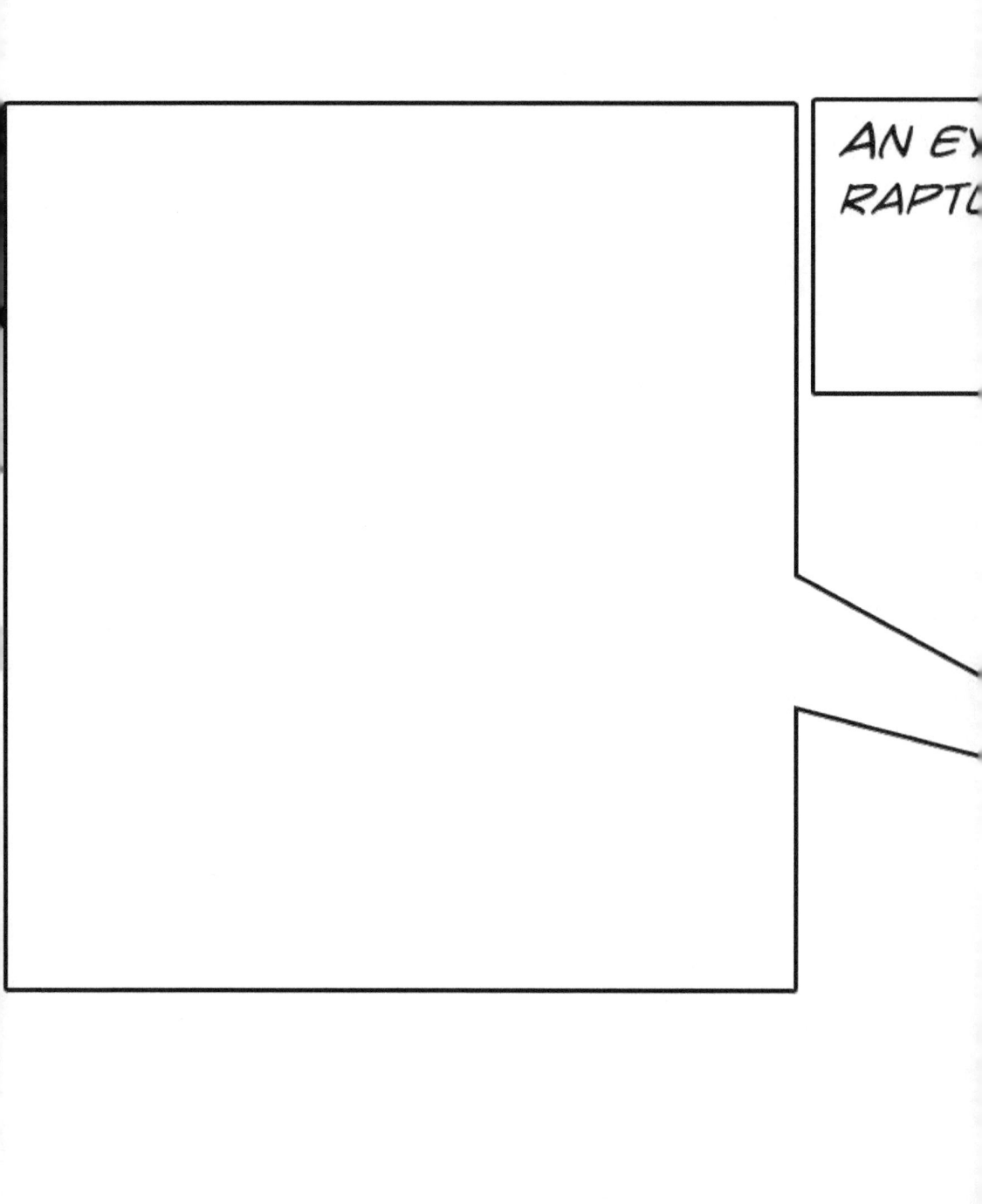

AN EY
RAPTO